AUTOMOTIVE EXCELLENCE

Exploring the Intuitive Art of Business Repetitive Excellence

By Siboniso Thwala

COPYRIGHT

TABLE OF CONTENTS

PREFACE

Embracing the responsibility and following the inner voice

We all want to live life for as long as we have intentions or plans for the future. The unavoidable part of this is that we cannot live the life we want without the existence of others; whether we like it or not or whether we like them or not, we don't have the choice to be alone. Someone else needs to exist out there for us to accomplish what we desire. For example; a buyer needs a seller and a seller needs a buyer. A seller embraces the responsibility to make available what the buyer doesn't have. The seller who not only embraces this responsibility, but also takes risks and uses initiative is classified as an entrepreneur.

Once these sellers, or entrepreneurs, gain success from their businesses they get tagged, or labelled, as extraordinary and are generally perceived to possess high intelligence. Fair enough, I respect and honour the ones that have made it to that level, but have we ever taken a moment to wonder whether it's not just entirely due to having an extraordinary IQ in comparison to the rest of us? Could it also be due to taking responsibility to fix wrongs, or to make things easier for others, or to enable the disabled?

We are all disabled to a degree. Show me a man who is able to do anything and everything that all unique individuals in the world can do. Even a "Jack of all trades" would take several lifetimes to attempt every known trade.

We all require the help of the enabled for the things we can't do. Thus it is those who make an effort to embrace the responsibility, of ensuring that we get help with what we need, who end up succeeding as extraordinary entrepreneurs.

- **Bill Gates** made the world happy; ok perhaps not his competitors, when he took computers to the friendliest level by designing the windows system. He made it his responsibility to change the unfriendliness of computers into something usable by everyone. Have you ever wondered how complex it was to use a computer prior to Windows? Was Bill Gates the only one with the ability to create a user-friendly system? Who knows, perhaps there was someone who could have done an even better job but never took the responsibility.

- **Larry Page and Sergey Brin** created Google search. Life today wouldn't be as easy without it. There are other people out there, who possess the same abilities that these two applied in creating Google search, but they didn't embrace the responsibility to make life easier for us as Larry and Sergey did.

I could go on about these extraordinary entrepreneurs, and believe me there are many out there, but I won't because this book is not about them. This book is about you and me, and specifically about how we can embrace our responsibility to become extraordinary entrepreneurs in the eyes of other people, and also perhaps reap the rewards of our efforts.

How many people would take on the responsibility of washing dead bodies? Yes, it's a difficult job but it's doable and essential. Not many would, preferring instead to try to be the next Bill Gates, forgetting that the world doesn't need a second Bill Gates and that there are many other complexities and problems that need to be solved.

Surely you've heard someone complaining about the delivery service for a pizza, then after that possibly even commenting about what needs to be done to improve the service. The sad part is that those people see the problems and the need. They may even have the solution but still choose to play it safe and leave the risk and hard work to someone else.

Isn't that intuition?

Isn't that Instinct?

They already know what should be done to make things right, but they don't trust that they can make the difference. They don't want the responsibility of enabling the disabled and becoming legendary in the eyes of others.

This is how you know that you are gifted. Yes, you are an entrepreneur!

How many things have you seen going wrong and falling apart and have thought of the ways to improve them, but never took a chance to put them into place?

If you've never took a chance, perhaps you have never trusted your inner voice.

"Today I will do what others won't, so that tomorrow I can accomplish what others can't" - Jerry Rice

The first step towards becoming an extraordinary entrepreneur is to take responsibility; to be prepared to do the things no-one else wants to do.

"Anyone can be an entrepreneur, if they embrace the responsibility to fix the wrongs and to enable the disabled" - Siboniso Thwala

In the first chapter we will further explore the importance of responsibility to the role of the entrepreneur. In the following chapters we will look at the other crucial factors.

How do you know that you are an entrepreneur?

That you have what it takes?

How do you choose the right business?

AUTHOR BACKGROUND

I'm a Quantitative Analyst, Business Researcher and an Entrepreneur.

As you begin this journey, let me tell you something about me and the events leading to the creation of this book.

I was born and raised in Soweto. I lived in a township called Jabulani until I reached my early twenties.

In my early life, before I finished high school, I was obsessed with only 2 things, debating and business knowledge. I became a leader of the debating team at my high school. Each day after school, when I got home, I would enjoy reading business magazines or watching business programs on TV.

Then in 2003, after I represented my school and conquered well in a "United Nations" themed debate held at Wits by the SAIIA, I was offered the opportunity to take up a bursary to study in the faculty of Humanities and so I convinced myself that I would study to be a teacher once I finished school.

I submitted my application to study towards a BA degree and once I'd completed Matric, it came time to hand in my results in order to complete the registration and commence the studies. But something felt wrong as I was standing in the queue at the registrations office; it felt as if I'd left something behind.

What was it? Where was it left? At home, at the door or in the taxi?

Well it turned out to be something abstract, so it couldn't have been left anywhere in the places I've mentioned.

It was my hunger to learn more about business, the hunger that I'd buried in mothballs since convincing myself that I was destined to be a school teacher.

I have no proclivity for giving up, but when that hunger resurrected I instantly gave up the offered opportunity to studying teaching. I remembered that I'd always promised myself that I would learn more about business and so I decided to enrol for ND: Banking at Unisa.

Fortunately, while I was doing my distance learning at Unisa, I secured a position in a call centre at MBD Attorneys collecting outstanding debts. I worked there for 2 years and 6 months and I learned the art of milking a stone; of collecting money where it seemed impossible. Then a wonderful colleague told me to apply for a job at FNB as he'd heard rumours that they had positions available.

To cut a long story short, I got a job at FNB as a call centre supervisor (Team Leader), where I started to gain more business knowledge from managing people. In 2012, after I had learned more about computer programming, I further advanced my career to become an analyst. The computer programming knowledge turned out to be very useful when analysing massive values in the form of money.

Currently I continue to serve the bank as an analyst. I analyse trends and performances, offer advice and tell stories with numbers to my stakeholders, who are primarily managers of various departments. I assist them to make informed decisions and give advice where I can.

Outside of the Bank, I run various small businesses due to my inquisitiveness and out of a passion to advance myself and gain knowledge.

Enough about me, moving on I would like to say thank you to my family, all the people that have given me opportunities and the ones that are still playing a role in helping me on my journey.

I would especially like to mention the other two most important people who have made it possible for me to succeed in writing this book.

Lara Katharine Stander, a special lady, a writer, friend and editor of this book. I'm a big fan and I admire the work and the contributions which you made to the anthology entitled, "Whispers of a Dying Flame", as well as the other work that you shared with me which is to be published in future. Thank you so much for your help, each day I learn a lot from you and I wish you all the best in your endeavours toward success.

Tiisetso Maloma from www.bulabuka.co.za. A young, dedicated businessman and friend, who helped me tremendously and offered guidance through his writing experience. Congratulations on your 3rd book "The Anxious Entrepreneur".

Is it that easy to commit to taking up responsibility and managing it?

Sometimes it's not.

But there is an easy system for understanding how to manage your responsibility.

One word makes it clear.

ROLE

1. ENTREPRENEURSHIP IS ROLE PLAYING

Everyone is someone to somebody; a sister, a brother, a wife, a father, and so on. These are roles which are an essential part of our lives.

How do your customers see you?

What are you to them?

Do you create an experience that makes them look forward to experiencing the same again tomorrow?

Do you create that experience which plays an essential role in their lives?

In this section I would like to pick the role of a father to highlight the importance of playing a good role.

ROLE PLAYING IS ABOUT SERVING A NEED AND CLOSING A GAP

When I entered fatherhood, I became a father not just by having a baby but by fitting the role and closing a gap. Fitting this role involved a lot of things, some to which it was easy to adapt and others which were more challenging and brought sacrifices. In fitting any role, you need to do things as demanded by the role and the most challenging ones are sacrifice and endurance. These sacrifices involved things like stricter budgeting, changing nappies, putting my needs aside and so on. Changing nappies is a good example of something which cannot be done only whenever it suits you, but has to be done when meeting the need is demanded by the baby.

In the same way, when you connect in a relationship with a customer, you're not just selling a breakfast, lunch, snack or dinner, but you are serving a need when required. You are taking up a challenge according to your customer needs. You are embracing the responsibility to do what you need to do to make things better; to find a solution or to solve a problem. By playing your role properly and responding to the demands in an appropriate way and in the right time, you gain the advantage of being offered a role in your client's life.

There's always a first time for everything, likewise your customers will have a first time experience with your product (in this instance, food). If a customer has a first experience that satisfies, or even exceeds, his expectations, he is likely to return to repeat the experience because he realised a potential in you to fulfil a role in his life. In other words, your ability creates a dependency and makes you important.

Let me draw two examples here to link your service to a beneficial role in a client's life.

Example 1

IT'S A HEALTHY MEAL: Craig Fowler, who works at a municipal office, drives a 2km distance every day to buy lunch from Rose Takeaways. The municipal office has a canteen, which sells food to staff during lunch-time, but the food is greasy and unhealthy, so Craig prefers the inconvenience of driving to Rose's where he can get a meal to fit his dietary requirements. Now Rose is not just selling a lunch meal to Craig, but she is adding value in his life and helping him to accomplish his fitness plan.

Example 2

RELEVANCE TO THE SCHEDULE: Nomsa is a single parent of two boys. Her elder son, aged 14, is at high school and the younger, aged 7, is at primary school. Because she has to drive the boys to separate schools before heading for work, Nomsa has no time to prepare a proper breakfast for them in the morning. Her solution is to make her first stop, after leaving the house, at Rose Takeaways. She has built a good relationship with Rose who makes it a priority to prepare breakfast for her in time every day. Rose has therefore become a vital part of Nomsa's life, by meeting both her need to save time and to get a proper nutritional start to the day.

WHAT ARE THE CRUCIAL THINGS OF WHICH AN ENTREPRENEUR NEEDS TO TAKE ADVANTAGE IN ORDER TO BE A GOOD ROLE PLAYER?

Psychological research indicates that over 80% of people in the world have a low self esteem, so boost their esteem.

Have you ever considered how many times people buy things that they don't need just to feel better, to prove a point to someone, to gain recognition, to fit in to a certain group and so on?

Why is that?

Siboniso Thwala

One day there was a special event for school children in Soweto. It was a big event, which hosted several well-known music artists and motivational speakers, who had been invited to entertain and inspire the students.

As I had already been in the catering industry for some time, I was invited to attend as one of the food vendors. I had, however, underestimated the competition and I wasn't getting enough support from the students. They were buying from the people they knew.

I despaired of selling much until my friend, who was helping me for the day, gave me a wakeup call by commenting that the singers must be hungry after so many hours of singing. The idea hit me like a ton of bricks and I rushed to prepare food for the singers, taking a risk, not knowing if they would eat my food or not. Fortunately after I offered, they came one by one to get food from my stand.

By the time each of the four singers had taken a break and eaten my food, all my stock was gone.

Now I'm sure I know what you're thinking. You must be thinking that it's impossible for four people to finish all my stock for the event, and you would be right.

It's not that the four celebrities managed to finish all my stock by themselves, but that once they were seen sitting under my umbrella and eating my food, other people also became interested in what I had to offer.

Did I succeed that day, to sell all my stock, merely because of the fact that all four of the people who had the most attention from the audience ate my food?

The answer is no!

I succeeded because people have low self-esteem.

For two hours during the concert I had been struggling to convince people to buy. It's not that they weren't interested; it's that they were only interested in my food to the same degree as to that of my competitors. (I was selling pretty much the same things as everyone else after all). But, as soon as they saw people with high profiles eating my food, they became more interested. Then they came in numbers, because they wanted to be seen buying the same food that was bought by the celebrities.

Why did they become more interested?

Because people have low self-esteem, they seek approval from those they look up to.

For example; if a young person sees his or her role model behaving or dressing a certain way, they are very likely to act and dress the same way, without doubt or fear of embarrassment, no matter how outrageous it may be.

- In the same way, a man seeking approval from his friends may enter a strip club, despite the fact that he may have been raised by a pastor who taught him never to set foot in such a place. He would be prepared to go against his upbringing, in order to fit in and gain recognition from his peers.

Low self-esteem is a big problem and causes many difficulties in society. Enterprising entrepreneurs however, know that it exists and how to take advantage of it. This is the reason big companies use celebrities as brand ambassadors for their products. They know that consumers are more likely to buy products endorsed by their heroes; people they recognise and trust.

Understand the impact of your failure to deliver

In the beginning I mentioned the role of a father; now I would like to link that role more closely to the role of the customer. A child stands a better chance of having a good life, if the father ensures that his role is played correctly. It's vital for a father to support his children with their visions, goals and purposes in life. In the same way, you stand a better chance of giving very good customer service if you understand important things about your customer, like the consequences they will suffer if you fail to deliver on their expectations.

You will never convince people of your impact in their lives if you cannot align your actions to what they deserve

Do you ever ask yourself why so many businesses nowadays want your contact phone number, email address or even physical address? The reason is because they want to optimize on their role in your life as a customer. These days if you go to a clothing shop to buy a jacket using cash, not even intending to open an account, they are likely to ask for permission to send you information regarding their specials and sales in future. They might frequently send you messages encouraging you to apply for an account in their store.

These actions could indicate that they care about making a difference in your life. This tactic also gains the business the advantage of making you aware of the potential role that they could be playing in your life. What type of role could this be?

Well, they know that it's not easy for most people to always have cash available, for when they are in need of something; some days are better than others and some are worse. The general need for credit has become a predictable fact of life which creates opportunity for businesses to take advantage of it. Notice, I use the word *need*.

I use the word *need* because people are more likely to act when they need something as opposed to merely wanting it. For example; you need to buy a school uniform in January, but you have no cash left due to over-spending during the festive season. This will be the opportunity for the clothing store to play their role, by assisting you to open an account and by giving you credit for the items you need to buy. Like a father, and again I would like to link this, the clothing store is providing a service that will improve your situation at your time of need, which then simply comes down to playing a role in your life.

As previously mentioned, playing a good role comes with sacrifices; that's always the nature of the challenge that comes with roles. In any business venture, you will need to make sacrifices to satisfy your customer needs. For example; some customers only get a 30 minute lunch break, which may not be enough time for you to prepare the food, serve them and still allow them enough time to eat. This might then require you to make the sacrifice of hiring extra help in order to speed things up.

Roles are very important; every successful relationship is driven by meaningful role-play between the people involved. So too, for a business to be successful it must fit into relationship by playing a meaningful role. To achieve this you need to understand that you are not just a food vendor. Once you realise that, you will maintain a good and lasting relationship with the client.

Siboniso Thwala

The border gate was so cruel to me

Sometime in my life, during a festive season, I visited Mozambique. When I arrived at the boarder gate, the temperature had already reached 42 degrees Celsius. The queue was extremely long, because of all the holiday travellers, so I spent 7 hours waiting in the queue just to get my passport stamped. For the sake of clarity and harmony, note that I'm not writing about this with the intention of blaming either the South African or Mozambique governments for anything; I'm writing it with the intention to expand on the topic of the chapter, which is your role in the life of a client. There are many people crossing borders during the festive season, which makes it difficult to get everyone across in a short space of time. When I say that the border gate was cruel to me, I say it because of the climate conditions; having to endure the long queues in the excessive heat with a dire lack of necessary resources and services.

While I was waiting in the queue, I noticed that several resourceful people, who were obviously familiar with the place and the conditions, were taking advantage of the situation. They were selling water, which under normal conditions would be taken for granted, but under these conditions was more valuable than gold. The heat there, in mid-summer, is so intense that you are completely soaked in sweat and constantly thirsty. I witnessed a 5 year old child screaming and shouting at her mom, crying for water and ice cream like a drug addict in withdrawal.

Of all the people selling water, there were two kids who stood out even more. They were undeniably impressive as they came to my rescue like angels. I was battling with the internet connection; I needed to transfer money from my savings account to my cheque account, as I didn't have my savings account card with me. I didn't have cash on me because I had intended to withdraw money once I arrived at the border gate and hence, was totally unprepared for the situation. So I suffered the consequences of not thinking ahead.

It was after I had stood in line for about 4 hours with no water and my body covered in sweat when, out of the blue, two young boys spoke to me. They told me that they had noticed that I'd been sweating a lot and standing for a long time without drinking any water. I explained my situation to them, that I was battling with the internet connection and I couldn't withdraw cash from my account.

They saved me the embarrassment of collapsing in front of everyone! Instead of leaving me to my fate, as they could have done, they offered me a 1 litre bottle of water, a cell phone to do my transfer and lent me an umbrella. Eventually when I was able to draw money, I paid them and then also gave them a good tip.

My lesson from this was that they were able to put themselves in my shoes. In addition to that, they went over and above my expectations; first, by taking the risk of trusting me by giving me water without immediate payment; second, by helping me to get my money by organizing a cell phone for me and third, by lending me an umbrella to make my wait, under the blazing sun, a little more comfortable. Today I write this chapter, about the service provider's role in the life of the client, because of them. They played a very important role in my life that day, merely by assessing my need and then providing excellent service.

In short, they enabled me.

What role do you play in your client's life? Are you one of those people who care only about the bottom line? If you've never asked yourself these questions, then you are at risk of losing your clients.

The story of the Border gate now brings me to the most important part of this chapter.

People only remember how you make them feel, not what you have done for them

We remember our parents and guardians when we are far from them, or when they pass away, because of the way they made us feel when we were young and in need of them. We remember our favourite teachers; because of how easily they helped us understand what was important for us to learn and how they gave us courage to learn, no matter how difficult it was. We remember our enemies because of how they terrified us, or spoiled our happiness, on one or more occasion. We remember our first kiss, because of the closeness and satisfaction we felt, after wondering for a lifetime how it would feel to do it. And we remember our heroes, because of the hope they inspire during the difficult times.

The two heroes that approached me at the Border gate, made me feel wanted and cared for in my time of need; despite the language barrier and despite the fact that I had no immediate cash to compensate them for their efforts. They believed my story about the challenges I was experiencing and offered the help no-one else would.

If I was in the same place today, with cash in my pocket, I would choose to buy from them again. I would ignore all the other people selling similar products and look for them, because they were the ones who made an impact and played a major role in my life that day. I would ensure that I dedicated my last cent to them if I was in the same space again, just because they made me feel special and cared for.

CONCLUSION

The duty of an entrepreneur is to make things easier in the life of a customer.

Every day, customers are counting on us as entrepreneurs and hoping that we will have an impact in their lives.

It's impossible to please a customer if you don't create an experience.

We, as entrepreneurs, need to create products and services that boost the self-esteem of our customers.

The examples of Craig Fowler and Nomsa, illustrate that entrepreneurship is about embracing the responsibility to enable the disabled.

- Craig is disabled in being unable to get a healthy meal, so he chooses to make the drive to Rose to enable himself to get what he needs.
- Nomsa is disabled due to her tight schedule, so she enables herself by relying on Rose to assist her in meeting all her responsibilities.

2. THE LINKS OF EXTRAORDINARY ENTREPRENEURSHIP

Now we have found our purpose in the world by embracing responsibility and we understand that we have a role to play in enabling the disabled and a duty to change their experience by making things easier. The next thing is to understand the strong links that keep extraordinary entrepreneurs effective.

The chart below depicts all the components important for successful entrepreneurship.

Embracing responsibility and playing a role, are only two components in the links which give us direction on how to begin the journey of being extraordinary.

Moving forward, we will look at the remaining components. These are the things which ultimately keep us in the industry.

CHECKLIST

i. **Embracing Responsibility** ✔

ii.   Playing a role   ✔
iii.   Managing your brain
iv.   Building and looking after strategies
v.   Understanding the secrets of wealth
vi.   Understanding simple investments
vii.   Looking forward to the future

You might already be getting the first two links right.

That of your responsibility and role.

Well done to you if you have.

But I assure you that some days are better and some are worse.

The sad truth is that we are human beings who feel pain during bad times.

[Managing your brain]

3. BALANCING STEREOTYPES, EMOTIONS AND RATIONALITY

The most powerful muscle in the human body is the brain. Like any muscle, the brain needs to be well looked after and exercised correctly. If not exercised correctly, the muscle may get stiff or even become damaged.

STEREOTYPES

During 2012 and 2013, I ran a computer business and had a really reliable supplier. His honesty and commitment contributed towards the success of my business. Not once did he ever fail to live up to his promises, he never sold me anything which didn't work and never showed any greedy intentions. His computers were always completely legit. I can say with confidence that I summed the man up as an honest, hard-working guy.

In addition to that mentioned above, I was also well aware, from the beginning of our relationship, that John was a foreigner. But we will come back to that.

Teaching yourself to judge people by their actions and basing your judgment on facts is very rewarding, especially when you are determined to make success of your business. Stereotypes, on the other hand, are the cancers which hamper the growth of our success.

What are stereotypes?
They are oversimplified conceptions, perceptions, opinions or beliefs about someone or something.

Example (Gender stereotypes):
Most men value fancy cars over family and marriage. In contrast, most women are dedicated to being significant parents to their children. A man would choose to have a fancy car rather than to buy his wife and kids a fancy house, while his woman longs for a beautiful home in which to nurture her family.

Although we all know that there are exceptions, why is this so often the truth?

It is because we are the product of our past. Period!

Early life: During his childhood, a young boy will be given toys to play with and typically, many of those toys will be cars. In addition, all of his friends will have toy cars and every day they will play, and compete, with each other. They will each show off the toy cars that their parents bought for them. Some will have bigger cars, some smaller cars and some will have electronic cars controlled by remote devices. In contrast, a young girl is given different types of dolls, to play with, compete with, and show off to her friends.

Adult hood: When boys grow up to be men, they take this to a higher level by buying real cars, expensive cars, to show off to their friends. Many men will put their cars first, before their wives and families. And so, many women are left as single parents and sadly enough, even if they get married to their children's fathers, they are not assisted with changing diapers or even with simple things such as bathing their babies. Much of this adulthood behaviour comes as a result of the stereotypes that were instilled from an early age. There is no law that says that little boys must play with cars and girls must play with dolls. Yet we choose to follow these stereotypes that have been the norm for generations.

Now back to business.

Business is like science, and science works on facts and what has been proven to exist. Therefore no business decision should be based on stereotypes.

A common saying, which I hear often, is, "don't judge a book by its cover". Thus, never make decisions based purely on face value, always reason based on facts and you will make good decisions. Your decisions on how to choose a reliable supplier, or hire a good employee, or offer a service which is relevant to everyday life, should therefore not be based on stereotypes or emotions.

In my own experience, I have heard many stories and rumours about foreigners committing crimes, scams and a variety of illegal activities. Had I based my decision in choosing, or not choosing, a supplier based on this stereotype, who knows how many losses I may have suffered in my computer business?

By choosing to use John, I created a winning formula by taking advantage of the fact that many people didn't trust him and also were afraid to go all the way into Hillbrow; a proclaimed "Rough side of Town". In some instances he would sell some of his stock to me very cheaply, due to pressures of having to get rid of stock, so he could pay his rent and cover the running costs of his business.

You could also establish a winning formula by taking advantage of such stereotypes and other factors; bearing in mind that none of it should ever involve any illegal activities.

THE EMOTIONAL CONTROLLER

We all have emotions and sometimes we experience bad emotions that can be simply explained as frustration. Occasionally, we get frustrated in such a way that we can't pinpoint the origin of our frustrations. Customers, employees, suppliers and any people that you work with in your day-to-day business will be emotional at some stage. And so will you.

The study of psychology says that the brain is controlled by two components; the **Emotional component** and the **Rational component.**

The emotional ruler is about feelings and imagination. The rational ruler is about logic (which is reasoning with, or according to, validity). Hence, logic is all about understanding and knowledge, whereas the emotional component enjoys comfort over reasoning.

Knowing (associated with the rational ruler) and feeling (associated with the emotional ruler) are linked very closely to each other, but we are generally unaware of this, to the extent that often we form our thoughts according to our feelings and so create 'knowledge' from emotions.

As I said earlier, the brain is a muscle and if emotion, especially negative emotion, is overused, the brain becomes tired and worse; it gets damaged. The sad part is that we train our brains to think in a certain way, without realising we are doing it. In the end, this causes us to be over-emotional and leads to failure.

Imagine watching a movie about a foreigner enslaving and killing the people of your country. The movie is based on a true story which occurred in 1978. You see blood and tears everywhere; from the beginning to the end of the movie. Soon, your emotion kicks in and you start to imagine the pain that your fellow brothers and sisters felt. Then, before you know it, you imagine this happening to you or your family; feeling the pain as if you had personal experience of the incident. Your imagination will impact you to such an extent, that you will think you know how it feels to suffer the same pain. In worst case scenarios, you may then allow that emotion to overpower your personal and business decisions about foreigners.

Later in this chapter, to prove the power of emotion on brain development, we will look at the story of a woman by the name of Suze who developed negative knowledge in her mind about herself, because of emotional suffering. In the end, she overcame her negative beliefs and false knowledge by being rational (reasoning and validating).

There are many instances of people in business, finding themselves facing challenges, who end up allowing their emotions to make the final decision. How many businesses have closed down because the owners have decided to call it quits, preferring to go back to their safer, more comfortable, routines due to emotional overload?

Example

An attorney, who has worked for a law firm (ZTS Attorneys) for 6 years, decides to resign from his job to open his own law firm. His employer tries to convince him not to resign, because he is a greatly experienced attorney who does his job very well. Even though his boss begs him to stay, he decides that it's time to move on and start his own company. After he starts his company, he discovers pressures of running a business that he was never aware of.

Let's go back to the days when he used to work for ZTS. He would start off his day by having coffee with his colleagues, then he would surf the internet for a while, often he would download a few things using the company's computer and data. After that, he would attend to his job. During the course of the day, he would travel to the courthouse to deliver files; he had a petrol allowance which was paid for by the company. After dropping off and picking up files from court, he would pass by his girlfriend's place of work to have lunch with her.

Now let's return to the present day, when he owns his own law firm. He suddenly realises that he has lost the privilege of downloading things for free. Now all the data he uses is affecting him directly, as he has the pressure and responsibility of sustaining liquidity for his company. He must also cut down on any unnecessary travelling, as he now pays for his own petrol. On top of that, every morning he now has to sacrifice the prolonged tea times that he used to take, because of the pressure of running the business and making sure that all the work is done on time.

All the pressure is giving him mixed signals and emotions and he realises that it was much easier, and a lot more comfortable, when he used to work for ZTS. After a few months, he closes the business down and hopes that his previous employers at ZTS would still appreciate having him back. This attorney has concluded in his mind that he will not make it in his business because;

- he misses the comfort of working for his previous employer;
- e is emotionally drained by challenges he didn't prepare for and therefore concludes that his business will never be good enough, in the long run, to give him the luxury he had while working for ZTS attorneys.

RISKS IMPOSED BY EMOTIONS & STEREOTYPES

(a). Bad sales pitch

If you've ever sold anything in your life, either while being employed as a sales representative, or just selling something you personally own as a second-hand product, you would realise that it can, at times, be painful to be under pressure to sell something that people don't want to buy. Well, the reason you're feeling all this pain and pressure could be due to the fact that people are not buying because your focus is wrong; if your focus is not on solving a problem for your customer, but rather only on the feeling you will achieve once you attain victory through your sales pitch. The feeling that is linked to the satisfaction you long for; the emotion of achievement after a successful sale. So, the desire for this emotion causes damage to your interpretation of the service, or product, that you are selling and interferes with the process you should follow, in order to correctly promote the features and usefulness of the service or product.

(b). Emotion vs. Information

Strong emotions wipe information from the brain, causing poor attention to detail.

Take, for example, a lady selling food who is having a bad day. She tries to cook the ordinary meal that she serves to her clients every day. But because today she is stressed, she lacks focus and is paying less attention to detail, so doesn't mix the spices very well. Not that she doesn't know what she is doing; she knows very well, she has all the information on what to do and how to cook the meal. But because of the strong emotion, the information is suppressed. The results of this incident now cause her clients to complain about the food that tastes bad. Some clients could decide that they will no longer buy her food; others may be more lenient, in accepting that the lady made an error in not cooking the meal correctly, yet will still request to be refunded their money. She thus loses money, not only by having to reimburse the clients who are complaining, but also through reputational loss, as word gets out to other clients that the food she is selling tastes bad and so people don't even bother to try her meals any more.

(c). Unrealistic expectations – unrealistic goals

When I started in the food industry, in Johannesburg South, I was very positive and passionate. I was excited about the smooth operation that I anticipated, as my business was situated in a busy car wash.

I hadn't seen the need to be hands on, so it was only after some time that I realised that the business was not going well. I had taken things for granted; I'd believed, because the area was busy, that there would be no need for me to be too involved and that all I needed to do was hire people who would look after things.

Well I was wrong, very wrong! I had totally misjudged the situation.

Yes, the place was busy, but I didn't do a proper case study of the environment, or do my SWOT analysis very well (SWOT analysis is discussed in detail in the following chapter). The excitement and anticipation of success had taken over my thinking. I later found out that, although people liked to wash their cars in our car wash, they preferred to buy food from the local shops that were on the next street. Unfortunately, I was never made aware of these shops and had expected people to buy my food while waiting for their cars to be washed. I didn't account for the fact that they bought food from these local shops *before* coming to the car wash. Another problem was that, because I hadn't done a proper analysis, I failed to realise beforehand, that the food that I was selling was exactly the same as that which was sold at the local shops which the customers were used to. I had bought too much stock and had to give some of it away after the first week of business, as the food was rotting. Although I continued on for several weeks after that, spending money on new stock and hoping the situation would change, I failed. When I did the analysis it was already too late. The expenses killed my passion and my hopes were fading. I still had to pay salaries, as well as maintain the rent, even though I was not coming close to the break-even point.

Yes, these are the results of unrealistic expectations, due to rushing in the excitement of making money. But I have learned my lesson and will never make the same mistakes again. I now know that I need to set realistic expectations, based on properly analyzing the facts. In that way, I will guarantee realistic expectations, set proper goals and avoid failure.

This is why realistically, in the accounting perspective, businesses are required to stipulate provisions and apply depreciation methods. Having 20 people who owe you money doesn't necessarily mean all of them will pay you; you need to allow for the provisioning percentage of the estimated people that possibly won't pay you as your provision for bad debts. You also need to take into consideration that your most valuable asset, which you purchased for $15 000, will not retain its value over time. You need to account for the fact that you will not be able to sell the item for the same amount after 5 years of use. By doing even these things, you are beginning to set realistic expectations.

(d).   Fear of letting go due to emotional attachment - The cause of unfinished projects

At times we will engage in a project which we do very well, a project to which we give our all and on which we enjoy working every day. We may even enjoy it so much that we turn it into a hobby.

But, have you ever started these projects and failed to finish them? Failed to finish them, but not because you are incompetent or unable to finish them? I used to have those problems, until I did some research as to why this was happening.

I was advised, by someone who is well versed in psychology, that the reason for not being able to finish these projects is a common problem caused by the fear of letting go of what we enjoy doing.

DEALING WITH EMOTIONAL RULERS & STEREOTYPING

(a).   Find the origin of the emotion

It is always better to know what makes you angry, pinpoint its origin and deal with it, even if it means brainstorming and writing down all the events which led to your frustration. My story about the food business in the car wash should shed some light on the issue and give an example of how situations can affect us. Everything in a business venture must be analysed before any decisions are taken. No matter how positive and happy you are about something, you need to realise the importance of understanding the drive behind that happiness; is it real, or just imagination? The same applies with an emotion resulting in anger. Try to figure out why you are angry before giving in to the emotion.

(b). When ruled by emotion, delegation is the best tool

It's an unfortunate fact that we sometimes become emotional under stress and are unable to perform competently at work. In such instances, it's best to delegate your tasks to someone with the experience and skill that may be needed by a customer.

In the same way, if you have an employee who is struggling with an emotional issue, you should delegate their tasks to a competent person and allow them time to deal with the matter and recover before carrying on with business.

(c). Before accepting a stereotype, ask yourself why

Stereotypes often come from myths or stories that we have been told by other people. They are based on judgments made by people about other groups of people. Sometimes these judgments are made because of bad experiences and in worst cases, they originate from racial prejudice. The best judgments, leading to successful decisions, are based on facts. When you are making a decision that will impact your future and/or the future of your business, it is always best to confirm with yourself *why* you are making that decision; make sure your decision is based on thorough investigation rather than acceptance of the norm.

(d). Breaking free from stereotypes- get a second opinion

Although stereotyping helps society function by categorising groups of people, what they do and what we can expect of them (let's use firemen as an example), accepting any stereotype as an absolute is dangerous and doesn't allow for growth. Your catering business does not have to be a carbon-copy of MacDonald's in order to succeed; no-one is the same; that is why we are called individuals.

We cannot, however, do everything ourselves. Many small business owners prefer to make all the decisions and do everything themselves, forgetting that no-one can be perfect at everything, or know everything. At times, it is good to get a different perspective on things and to consult with those who have more experience. This is very important, especially when you are still new in business. Even experienced Medical practitioners often refer you to a specialist when faced with an issue that is beyond their scope.

To conclude this topic, let me share with you the story of someone who overcame the stereotypes and emotional rulers to become a successful businesswoman. Her story may perhaps shed some light on how emotions and stereotypes hinder us on our path to success.

THE STORY OF SUZE ORMAN

If there's one person whom I respect for overcoming stereotypes and the emotional ruler, to end up as a successful businesswoman, it's got to be Suze Orman.

Suze Orman had speech problems while growing up. She referred to herself as a child who suffered the emotion of secretly feeling dumb, a child who always scored among the lowest in the class. In her childhood years, she constantly had this feeling haunting her. After High school, when she applied at the University of Illinois at Urbana-Champaign to study towards becoming a brain surgeon, a guidance councillor advised her to try studying something simpler. Although Suze took this advice and changed her major to social work, she still failed to graduate in 1973; the degree was withheld due to her failure to fulfil the language requirements for the course. This failure seemed to further validate her emotional belief about herself so she left without her degree.

She eventually found a job as a waitress in a bakery, where she worked for 6 years. While working there, she shared her dream of owning her own restaurant with one of her regular customers; Fred Hasbrook. Fred undertook to help her raise funds towards this venture and with his help she managed to raise a sum of $50 000.00. He advised her to invest the money until she had enough to start her restaurant, so she approached a broker to assist her.

Although she advised the broker that she earned a low salary and needed to keep the money safe, he persuaded her to give him control over her funds and then pursued a risky strategy which resulted in her losing the money within 3 months. After this incident, Suze took an interest in learning more about investments and then applied for a job as a broker at the same firm where she had lost her money. During her training there, she discovered that the broker had violated the policies of the company but got away with it as he made a lot of money for the company.

This injustice pushed Suze into getting out of her comfort zone and she made the decision to sue her employer for the money she had lost. According to law, the company was unable to fire her and they ended up settling with her out of court.

As Suze explains; she made the decision to go against the company she was working for because she had nothing to lose. I say she validated facts! It wouldn't have helped her to fail to take action because she feared the results of taking a risk. Giving in to imagination creates failure.

THE REWARDS OF REALITY

Now let's look at facts vs. imagination in this case.

If Suze had allowed the emotion of fear to rule her mind;

- she may still have been working for the same company which cheated her,
- she may have ended up as a waitress for the rest of her life,
- she may still have been telling the story that she could have been a businesswoman if it wasn't for the greedy stock broker who cheated her out of her money.

Because of the facts and logic that Suze followed;

- she is currently an author, a television personality, a motivational speaker, a businesswoman, a financial advisor and an investor.

CONCLUSION

There is no room for stereotypes in the mind of a businessman / businesswoman.

By avoiding stereotypes you stand a better chance of growing as an entrepreneur and as a person in general.

Emotions cannot be avoided, but what we can do is deal with them. A healthy balance between business and emotion must be maintained.

By practicing emotional intelligence, you better your chances of building long lasting relationships.

CHECKLIST

i.   **Embracing Responsibility**   ✔
ii.   **Playing a role**   ✔
iii. **Managing your brain**   ✔
iv.   **Building and looking after strategies**
v.   **Understanding the secrets of wealth**
vi.   **Understanding simple investments**
vii. **Looking forward to the future**

What is your number one asset?

Which is the asset which pays you big bucks?

Strategy.

4. BUILDING AND LOOKING AFTER STRATEGIES

Ants are highly strategic insects; they form colonies with specialised groups who work together to support the colony. Worker ants can live up to 3 years and a queen can live up to 30 years. To find food, the colonies send scouts who all go off in random directions, dropping pheromones (or chemical scents) to find their way back to the nest. Once food is found, the ant will lay a stronger scent on her trail back for other ants to find. Isn't this an amazing and lucrative strategy?

Whether you already have an existing business or are in the process of starting your own, you also need a strategy which will drive the success of your business, a strategy which will cover the gap between your desires and achievements and most importantly help your business to survive. Do you think that ants would live for up to 30 years if it wasn't for the good strategy they possess? Even if you already have a strategy for your existing business, you still need to understand the elements which are necessary and important to your strategy and how they relate to your daily life. Once you understand them, it will be much easier for you to come up with strategies to resolve any problem.

THE IMPORTANCE OF BUILDING A STRATEGY

Target gives birth to strategy, then strategy rewards target!

Let us first consider the definition of strategy; it is defined as a plan or pattern of actions, which is used as a means to get from where you are to where you want to go. Where you want to go is your target. I assure you that any business which is sustained by a target stands a better chance of survival. Once you have a target, it becomes simpler to apply your strategy. It becomes as simple as putting an address into your GPS, which in this situation is the means by which you will arrive at your target.

This topic brings me to the point where I'd like to share one of the memories that I hold close to my heart and that I treasure and truly honour.

On the 11th April 2001, after school, I discovered that there would be a big soccer match in the evening. There I was, so excited to hear this as I recognized a good business opportunity for myself. Trust me, I did not thumb suck the date, it was a big match, you can goggle it; this day left an impression in the memories of many South Africans. These were the days when I became addicted to business and began to take advantage of informal trading; I was on a mission to make some money for myself, also due to the situation I faced at home. As I was still at high school, I was unemployable but I needed money. So on this day, when the opportunity presented itself, I borrowed R200.00 from someone and purchased cigarettes. The soccer match was at Ellis Park Stadium, scheduled to start in the evening, and my plan was to sell the cigarettes at the stadium during the match.

Because of the pressure of having to repay the money which I had borrowed, the adrenalin was pumping high. I had to set targets and make sure that I sold all the cigarettes in order to at least cover the amount which I'd borrowed. So making a profit was my first priority; first target, and breaking-even; making back the money I had spent, was my second priority. So I had to come up with a strategy to help me achieve that.

I realised the advantage of travelling by train and made it a part of my strategy. It occurred to me that just sitting, doing nothing, while I waited to arrive at my destination would not help me. So I started selling cigarettes to the other passengers. I set a target to sell at least a quarter of my stock on the train, which would make the burden easier for me once I arrived at the stadium.

Lucky enough, the strategy worked and when I got to the stadium a quarter of my stock was sold. At the stadium it was even easier and I managed to sell everything before the match was over. I made more than 100% profit that evening, even managing to get home before everybody else left the stadium, which as it turns out may have saved my life as well. Unfortunately, this soccer event brought pain to the lives of many South Africans because there was a stampede which caused 43 deaths.

Big companies set targets for the entire financial year and then break them down to monthly targets, weekly targets and daily targets. For your strategies to add value, you should adopt the same approach. You can even break them down further and set milestones to achieving a portion of the target in an hour, or half an hour; whichever suits your goals.

But note that you don't have to limit yourself only to time tracking when setting your targets. For example; a man selling cigarettes, while moving around a stadium, can set a target to sell at least 2 cigarettes per group of 10 people. The statistics show that at least 20% of people in the US smoke, so 2 out of every 10 people. This means, that if I were selling cigarettes in the US environment, I would aim to have at least 2 potential clients from every group of 10. Get it? (2 ÷ 10 X 100). But remember, in using these techniques, you also need to apply facts. So make sure you do your research about the environment, the people, and the laws and so on. This now brings us to how you integrate these methods of applying facts when developing a strategy, once you have set a target.

ONCE I HAVE SET A TARGET, WHAT COMES NEXT?

(a).   You have options

"If you can't fly, then run,

If you can't run then walk,

If you can't walk then crawl,

But whatever you do, you have to keep moving forward."

– Martin Luther King Jr.

When faced with a tough situation, as you look around at the environment, the people and the situation, you are suddenly able to distinguish between what threatens you and what gives you courage and hope, and then the answers start to unfold. We are always afraid of the things which threaten us and put us at a disadvantage. But no matter how complex the situation is, we find ourselves able to find options to dig us out of the hole.

But can we just choose any option to solve our problems? No! The reason for this is that everything has both a good side and a bad side and we are not always equipped to take on everything. The above quote by Martin Luther King Jr. says this perfectly.

(b).   You choose your options by applying SWOT.

SWOT is short for Strengths, Weaknesses, Opportunities and Threats.

Strengths

Strengths are the abilities you possess. Let's just review abilities.

Abilities are what you do best; they can be skills or talents. They are what you can do more of, and sometimes better than, other people. Let's look at a few examples;

- The ability to detect quickly whether your customers are unhappy with your service
- The ability to rapidly build strong customer relationships
- The ability to relate to needs

Sometimes your advantage could be due to material things, like having a very large vehicle that is able to carry large quantities. Because of this, people may prefer for you to move their furniture, as you would only need to make one trip whereas other businesses may need to make several.

In the story I used as an example, I had the foresight to realise that I could sell some of my stock even before I reached the stadium. I realised too, that I had a commodity for which there was a general demand. I understood that cigarettes could be sold anywhere and that there were fewer people selling them on the train than in the

51

stadium. This was the strength on which I succeeded.

Weaknesses

Weaknesses are the opposite of strengths; they are what you don't possess or in which you are lacking. Below are the examples;

- Using old technology;
- Lack of a certain skill;
- Being short-staffed;
- Being new to the business and unknown to the market.

Did I mention the fact that I'm shy? No, I don't remember saying that. Well, if you have ever been on a train you will know that the people who have confidence walk everywhere, making noise about what they are selling to get attention. In the face of this, I had to overcome my weakness somehow. I did this by wearing a cardboard placard on which I wrote, "Cigarettes for R2.00". So, because I understood that my shyness was a disadvantage and thus the weakness in my strategy, I made a plan to overcome this in the most logical way I could think of and it paid off. I turned my weakness into a strength by realising that it was unlikely I would be heard above all the other noise in the train.

Before I continue any further, let me point out two important things of which you may not be aware; I've covered strengths and weaknesses as the first two components of a SWOT analysis. These two have something in common, as they are the components over which you have control when forming your strategy. The other two, which follow, are mostly dependent on economic and other conditions and at times they may force you to adjust your strategy when they are not in support of your goals.

Opportunities

These are advantages, to you or your business, which are not because of your actions or abilities, but due to situations. The economic situation is one example.

Further examples could be;

- The majority of the population of the country support a certain sport;
- The weather is in favour of your event;
- Your customers buy or avoid products due to religious beliefs; (eg; 80% of the community don't eat pork so you could focus on buying and selling chicken, which is cheaper and would provide you with a higher profit margin.)
- Your customers have a special day, in every calendar year, which they celebrate.
  I have noticed, and perhaps you too have noticed, that spending increases on special days or periods in specific areas.

One of the opportunities presented to me, in my story, was that I knew that the soccer match between the two teams that were playing was important to almost everyone. Also, in 2001 it was easy to be in business as an informal trader, so I took advantage of that as well. Another of the opportunities that I recognised was that I didn't have to sell my cigarettes at the regular price; you may have noticed that cigarettes are very expensive during such special events.

Threats

Threats are disadvantages to your business over which you have no control, but for which you may need to change your strategy. Examples of this may be;

- An increase in the price of your stock;
- Changes in Government rules and regulations which may affect your business;
- Strikes;
- Industry prices.

In my case this could have been a taxi strike, which may have resulted in people not being able to attend the soccer match and having to watch it on their televisions at home. This could have affected me really badly. I might have needed, either to freeze the whole operation, knowing that there would be fewer fans at the stadium, or been forced to sell the cigarettes at a cheaper price to cut my losses and try to break-even.

HOW TO MAINTAIN A LUCRATIVE STRATEGY

See strategy as an asset

For a business, assets can be property, stock or equipment. The fundamental importance about an asset is that it has economic value, meaning that it is convertible to cash. An asset value is not likely to stay the same, sometimes its value will go down and sometimes it will go up. This is why its value must be checked, or revaluated, from time to time.

Imagine you have a car which you use daily. This means you have an asset which adds value to your life, serves a purpose and takes you from point A to point B. Therefore it would worry you if the car broke down, or slowed down in its performance. So to prevent this, you would frequently monitor the car's condition to ensure that it continues to add value as it's meant to.

In the same way, your business strategy needs to be constantly reviewed to ensure it adds value to your business. And if there are any lose ends to tie up, fixes to be done, amendments to be made or improvements to implement, so be it. Many companies have suggestion boxes to get feedback from their customers; this is another way of making sure that what they are doing is in line with expectations from their clients. They will make improvements on their products, processes and even services based on the feedback they receive from their clients.

How do I keep my strategy I line with my goals?

After a long time of travelling to work by car, you decide to try travelling by bus. Surprisingly, after your first day on the bus, you notice a few things; the differences between travelling with your own car and travelling by bus. You realise that there are benefits to travelling by bus such as;

- cost effectiveness,
- having time to surf the internet on your phone,
- being able to socialise and meet people.

You realise all of these things because you measured the outcome; what you got out of travelling with the bus.

(a).   Measure the outcome

After the implementation of a strategy, the outcome must be measured to see how effective it is. This helps to keep your strategy useful and relevant to your needs.

Businesses these days request information about where their clients heard about them, especially first time buyers or new clients. For example; you sign an offer to purchase with an estate agent and you fill in a block next to "where did you hear about us?" This will require you to answer whether you discovered them from radio / TV / internet / word of mouth /or other. Your feedback will simply allow them to measure the impact of their marketing channels and strategy.

(b).   Do process mapping

I introduced this chapter by talking about ants and their strategy for finding food. If one ant, after bringing food, fails to go back to collect more food, it will still be easier for the other ants to continue with the task, even if they were not with the ant that first discovered the food. This is simply because they know that they must follow the pheromone trail left by the ant which discovered the food. This also shows us that the ant's strategy is process mapped. Allowing and giving opportunity for others to follow the same rules, in order to succeed in reaching the end goal or target. It's important for a strategy to be mapped and documented; to record all the details of what you do and the linear process to follow in order to reach the goal.

(c). Copy and paste the magic everywhere

After measuring the success and mapping the processes, you already know what works, so you need to spread the knowledge to your employees and/ or colleagues to make sure that the strategy is copied by everyone, in order to achieve the same intended goal.

After some time selling cigarettes at the stadium, I became a master at it. Eventually, I decided to multiply my strategies by taking two of my friends with me to teach them what to do. That actually worked well for me.

CHALLENGES THAT DESTROY STRATEGIES

(a). **Lack of understanding:** For someone who has employed other people to carry on some functions of his organization, the common challenge is that not all of those people will fully understand the strategy. When people don't understand what you expect from them, they cannot add value.

(b). **No progress report:** Strategy needs to be measured in order to see if it adds value. Note that the measurement doesn't need to occur at the end of the project. When a soccer team gets a half time break, the coach will review the strategy. He will make important adjustments by changing the strategy if necessary. If the strategy is working well, he will compliment and encourage the players to stick to the plan.

(c). **Lack of task ownership:** sometimes, especially when things go wrong or when the tasks are too challenging for people, they don't want to take ownership.

(d). **Resistance to change:** if there is one thing that threatens people the most, it is change. Change commonly gives us the fear of the unknown. People resist doing things that will put them at a disadvantage, or at risk in any way. Something you believe to be right, someone else may believe to be wrong. So you stand the risk of not working together towards the same goal if you don't share the same beliefs. Even you; the owner of the business and the strategies, might be resistant to change. You need to recognise that this problem is not limited only to your staff or associates.

CONCLUSION

Strategy is essential for survival; even ants are living proof of that.

Strategy is an empty vault without a specific target. Without a target, it serves no purpose. For a good strategy to exist, a target must be set first.

SWOT is imperative for reasoning and deciding whether a strategy is worth implementing.

Strategy is an asset, as it facilitates the income process and should be evaluated often to see if it still serves the purpose.

i.   After the strategy is measured, proven to be beneficial and documented, it should be shared within the business.

CHECKLIST

i.	**Embracing Responsibility**	✔
ii.	**Playing a role**	✔
iii.	**Managing your brain**	✔
iv.	**Building and looking after strategies**	✔
v.	**Understanding the secrets of wealth**	
vi.	**Understanding simple investments**	
vii.	**Looking forward to the future**	

Turn a stranger into a daily cash ATM.

5. YOUR WEALTH IS IN CUSTOMER RETENTION

When I was young, I had my own perceptions about wealth. I believed that wealthy people make more money and spend more money. I was under the impression that they could afford to waste. After some time of observing and learning, I discovered that I was entirely wrong; I learned that wealth is what you keep, not what you earn!

At times, due to luck or advantage, you may have thousands of customers supporting you. But if you neglect to maintain a high level of service, they are unlikely, or less likely, to return to buy your products or utilise your services. This talks directly to the customer experience that you create.

Customer retention is loyalty. How often do you remain loyal to people who have disappointed you? Not very often, from my own perspective; even if I have no other options to choose from, I would merely tolerate them for the sake of necessity.

But let's face reality. In the real world of business, there are many aspiring entrepreneurs and customers nearly always have the option to choose a more favourable alternative to tolerating a bad experience from you. In the end, you will be like a dog chasing its tail, working and sweating for no benefit and constantly hustling for new clients to make ends meet.

Example:

Terrence runs an Events company. He recently managed to sign a deal with a school, which has a high reputation in the area because of its standard of excellence. He was contracted to organise a graduation party. The school secretary had happened to come across his advert, when she checked on Google for an Events organizer in their area. The advert which secretary had seen on the internet had looked wonderful and seemed promising. It gave her hope that the event would be enjoyable for the students and would create a memorable experience for them.

Unfortunately, the event turned out to be a major fiasco. The food was tasteless and unappealing and the décor couldn't even be considered average, it was so poor. The students complained about the food and décor, as they had paid a lot of money to attend the event. The poor secretary had to carry the blame for the disaster, as she had been the one who had recommended Terrence to organize the event. Furthermore, the students spread the word about the poor service received and the secretary decided never again to employ the services of Terrence or his company.

Sadly enough, Terrence doesn't consider this situation to be of major impact to his business. Instead of learning from his mistakes, he feels that the loss of one customer won't have a major effect as he can still hustle for other clients.

I HATE THE TERM "HUSTLER" BECAUSE IT IS PERCEIVED TO BE A STRUGGLE

I hear a lot of entrepreneurs, especially the younger ones, saying this word over and over again. Please don't take me wrong, don't think that I'm a hater and please follow my logic in this.

- Business is not a hustle!
- It's a way to contribute to the food chain, a way to add the missing piece of a puzzle.
- It's the passion that we have to change the industries in which we choose to specialise.
- It's an opportunity for us to become legends as we improve the industry and standards of living.

Your customers are the wealth of your business and this means that any engagements that you have with them, shouldn't be perceived as a hustle, or struggle, or even a punishment. Do you realise how the word hustle is used in most cases?

- "The older students hustled newcomers for money."
- "She's hustling an old man for money." Doesn't this leave a bad image in your mind?
- "It was a hustle to get to work this morning."

The above examples show that a hustle is a struggle. Do you want to hustle forever?

Entrepreneurs must have a hunger to keep clients, over and above the desire to attract more in order to improve their profits. Most businesses remain stagnant because they don't retain customers. They only fight for survival, or in order to conclude a transaction with a client, they constantly hustle and hope to hustle for more tomorrow.

Never ending pain, or hustle, will only lead you into giving up! Nobody wants to take a beating forever. So forget about, "it's fine, I'll just hustle for other clients".

What happens tomorrow, if you are no longer able to speak and are never again able to make a sales pitch? How will you acquire new clients? The new clients that you find, from time to time, will not take you to the next level. Keeping/retaining your clients and ensuring that they keep spending their money on your business, will take you to the next level.

THERE IS A MAJOR DIFFERENCE BETWEEN A NEW CLIENT AND AN OLD CLIENT

New Customer vs. Old Customer

New Customer	Old Customer
It is costly to get a new customer. In most cases, it takes a lot of convincing and resources may be exhausted. Constant marketing has to be done.	Once the customer has a good experience, not as much convincing, or use of resources, is needed to conclude the next deal.
A new customer has many doubts so your business is unlikely to be recommended initially.	Once an old customer is satisfied, you have the advantage of positive word-of-mouth advertising, which costs you nothing extra.
New Customers have the fear of facing an unknown entity.	Old customers already know what to expect from you.
New customers are risky if you offer credit. You are constantly unsure of whether a new customer will pay and if they don't, it can often result in further losses due to legal expenses.	Even if an old customers struggles to pay, you have built a trust relationship where you can afford to offer leniency for a period, or in extreme cases, profit from previous deals with him could balance out your losses.
Also in credit sales, fraud is more likely from new customers. Fraudsters give false details in their applications, making it hard to trace them. Tracing costs cause further losses.	There is less chance of fraud from someone you know. In the off-chance that it does happen, you are more likely to have valid address and contact details.

WHY EXTRAORDINARY BUSINESSES HAVE MANY CUSTOMERS

There is a myth about famous successful businesses. People think that these extraordinary businesses were created by people with exceptionally high IQ levels.

But they are wrong! In truth, most of these extraordinary achievements don't come from high intelligence levels, but from vision and an unfailing determination and commitment to achieving those visions, despite any obstacles.

Successful entrepreneurs fail and often they fail miserably many times over. But their secret is that they don't kiss and make up with their mistakes, they learn from them. They never waver from pursuing the most important thing keeping them going; their vision.

Vision and charm

You have a vision, you know what you want to achieve and that is why you are an entrepreneur. So here are some things that successful entrepreneurs also keep in mind.

They understand the vision of wealth

Someone once gave me a wakeup call. He told me that it wouldn't be possible for a million dollars to exist, if the last cent didn't exist. If you remove one cent from a million dollars, the number changes to something less than a million and this means that you are no longer a millionaire. The lesson is, that even the little that you have shouldn't be taken for granted, because as little as it is; it is the beginning, or starting point, of something bigger and better.

I apply the same vision, of keeping and quantifying each cent towards accumulating a million, to the possible income from my customers. The total number of customers you have represents your potential cash flow.

Number of customers retained	Multiply by ----->	Product/ Service Bought Costing $1.00		Answer	Explanation
0	X		0	= $ 0	no clients = zero customers zero income
1	X		0	= $ 0	1 customer who doesn't buy = no income. An example would be; a retained customer who would like to buy again but currently can't afford to.
1	X		1	= $ 1.00	1 customer who only buys once = low income
2	X		2	= $ 4.00	2 or á few customers who buy few services = some income, but non satisfactory
1000	X		2	= $ 2,000.00	More customers retained = more income, even if they only buy a few products.

CUSTOMER RETENTION GIVES COMFORT AND PEACE OF MIND

At the point where you are certain of a customer base that frequently buys your products or services, you become comfortable. Because now you know that all your effort is not going to waste, you know your stock will not perish, you know your expenses are covered, you know that you are not waking up early for nothing and you know there is a future to look forward to.

AFTER THE VISION COMES THE CHARM

They Charm the money from your pocket; they don't hustle or force it out!

If you believe I'm wrong, why are there so many rich men in the world who are still single? Just because they are rich, it doesn't mean that they can afford to waste their money on any random person.

They are still waiting for the one that will charm them, the one with whom they will be prepared to share all their wealth.

It begins with trust!

- How often do you talk freely with strangers?
- Do you trust any random person who you just met?
- Do your customers trust you?

The trust equation (TRUST = B.R.A.T) Belief + Reliability + Ability + Truthfulness

When you trust someone, you believe that they are reliable, have the ability to do what you expect from them and are truthful in their dealings with you.

I will break down the above definition and I dare you to not only ask yourself the questions below, but more importantly, to try to get your customers' perception. You can do this, either by drawing up a feedback questionnaire or by having a suggestion box where customers can leave compliments or suggestions for improvement.

1. **Belief:** You should be eager to find out if your customers believe in you, your product and even your business as whole. If they do not, you need to find out why and then try to resolve the issue.

2. **Reliability:** This term is associated with consistency. Do you constantly perform to the best level or do you provide good service only when it suits you? Do you strive to deliver the same service consistently and at all times? Do you sometimes perform well and other times badly?

3. **Ability:** Are you always able to deliver to what is expected of you? Are your skills and resources good enough to do what is expected?

4. **Truthfulness:** Are you always truthful and honest? Do you just preach, but do not practice. I often see companies developing slogans which they do not live up to. Imagine a taxi business which has a slogan that says, "Driving you anywhere you want," but not practicing what they preach. When clients ask to be driven to a destination outside of town, the drivers complain and reply that they can't drive that far out of the area. The slogan is therefore false advertising as the company has no intention of truly living up to the promise that was made.

   Be careful, especially with slogans, because they play a major role in your customer retention strategies. Don't create slogans carelessly or out of desperation. Always keep in mind that you will be expected to deliver on the promises you make, so make sure that you can.

In the first chapter, I spoke about the role of an entrepreneur. I mentioned that psychological research shows that over 80% of people in the world have a low self-esteem and sometimes this prompts them to buy things to gain approval from someone they look up to. This also works in your favour through word-of-mouth advertising. If a person hears about your wonderful product, or service, from someone they trust or look up to, you will also immediately gain their trust.

- You can gain the trust of one person and others will then trust you for the mere fact that you are trusted by someone they trust.

- If one customer is retained and remains loyal to you, other customers; who trust your loyal customer, are also likely to remain loyal to you.

WHAT HAPPENS AFTER THE CHARMING?

Apply the ECA principle – Evolution, Campaigning, and Accessibility

- *Evolution*

Every living thing in this world including human beings is subject to evolution. Yes, who wants to live in the caves nowadays? No one wants to because the days for that life are far gone!

Evolution is transformation, a change which is hopefully for the better. Products change and other businesses in your industry are constantly striving to improve their services, by introducing new technology and setting new standards for delivering service. So you can't expect your clients to continue to rank you as number 1 forever, if you refuse to change with the times. You need to realise that what worked well yesterday, might not work as well tomorrow.

I remember when I wanted to buy a cell phone, after I got my first job, and someone advised me to go for one of the respected brands. She further recommended that I should never buy a cell phone which has the same brand name as a fridge, or a microwave. Back then, people would make you feel as if you were backward if you bought such brands. So, in order to be in cool, you had to buy brands like Nokia and Erickson.

Today, brands like Samsung, which were previously only well known for their kitchen appliances, are leading in the cell phone industry.

Why?

They are leading because they evolved and transformed the industry. They covered gaps that were not covered before and completely revolutionised the product. A phone is no longer just a phone; you can read a book on it, get directions, surf the internet, play games and take photos. These and countless other things which were never possible before. So, by enhancing a cell phone with a camera, they not only saved us money, but offered us the convenience of owning one product instead of having to buy two. We, as entrepreneurs, need to be constantly aware of what our competitors are offering and figuring out how we can outshine them. I call this "A good deed inspired by jealousy!"

- **Campaigns**

Campaigns are the best! They are a method of giving love and staying in touch with our supporters or customers.

Drive your campaigns in a way that encourages your customers to love you more by doing the following;

- Identify your most loyal customers and classify them as first priority (HIGH)
- Identify the average customers and classify them as second priority (MIDDLE)
- Identify the irregular supporters and classify them as third priority (LOW)

Now that you have classified your customers, you have a better idea who you are dealing with in each group. The next step is to communicate the benefits you have decided to offer each group in your campaign. You can choose any form of media to advertise your campaign, but make it relevant to what your customers are familiar with. It will be a worthless exercise, and a waste of resources, for you to use a newspaper if your target clients don't read a newspaper. Choose a platform that is suitable and which is most likely to reach the maximum number of clients. As an option in today's world, social media is invaluable and cost effective.

For your campaign to be a success, you need to make the LOW group aware of the benefits that you are offering to the MIDDLE and the HIGH groups. You also need to inform the MIDDLE group of what you are offering to the HIGH group, to inspire them to support you more. Lastly; don't forget to advise the HIGH and MIDDLE groups of the benefits being offered to the LOW group, so that they can see the difference. It will make them feel special!

- *Accessibility*

It's being available and contactable when needed.

Remember, now that you have made an impression, people will be interested in contacting you for more information. Make sure that you are contactable on all the contact platforms; social media, emails, telephone and face-to-face. It is still a good idea to add the personal touch of a face-to-face meeting; people feel honoured when they get to meet the face behind the miracle work and they feel special when they are given the time to be seen. Accessibility also enhances your clients trust. It gives comfort in that it allows them to voice their concerns, should they have any problems with your product and service. Also with so many people committing fraud, accessibility guarantees the validity of the business.

THE OBSTACLE TO YOUR BUSINESS WEALTH

"The customer is always right"

This is a big fat lie. Not all customers are right.

What about the customers who intentionally mess with your bread and butter by stealing, committing fraud, harassing or abusing you or your staff unnecessarily?

We have to change our perceptions sometimes and let go of the people who keep dragging us down, or holding us back. There is no need to waste resources, time, or energy on such customers.

If you think I'm wrong, why do you think big successful companies have such things as strict lending policies and return of goods policies?

Also, why do you think that musicians use copyright to protect their work? Does a customer have the right, by buying a CD to sell copies for his own profit?

All I'm saying is that it is a good thing to spend time and resources where it is appreciated, but be aware that there are customers that can destroy your business.

CONCLUSION

Commit to your vision, no matter what!

Fight for trust by fulfilling the elements of the trust equation.

Charm your clients well and work on retaining their patronage.

Remember the duty of an entrepreneur which is to change the industry and close the gaps.

CHECKLIST

i.	**Embracing Responsibility**	✔
ii.	**Playing a role**	✔
iii.	**Managing your brain**	✔
iv.	**Building and looking after strategies**	✔
v.	**Understanding the secrets of wealth**	✔
vi.	**Understanding simple investments**	
vii.	**Looking forward to the future**	

Everyone is singing the word

Investment

But they think that it only has to do with cash quantity.

[Understanding simple investments]

6. MONEY IS NOT THE ONLY THING YOU CAN INVEST OR INVEST IN

An investment is a process of growing the value of your money to make a profit. There are many ways to invest money. These ways vary from stocks and bonds to real estate, precious objects, like art or jewellery or even business.

Even we as people have value. Also, the ways of investing in ourselves vary in many ways. There is a strong link between what we offer to the world and the return we get back from it. The more knowledgeable, skilled, trustworthy, credible and capable we are, the more we can get in return for sharing some, or all of those qualities.

Successful and extraordinary entrepreneurs invest in themselves.

Example: A 22 year old lady, who has been interested in art since the age of 15, has been busy with research for the past 2 months. As part of the research, she has been buying art magazines and following blogs on social media, by various artists. Her research has helped her to discover the following things; though there are people buying art because of the colours, design and composition, the majority of art buyers purchase art because of the subject matter. So this means that people buy art mainly because of the message, or the impact that it makes on their feelings.

The research provides crucial information to our young artist, particularly because of the fact that she has a wonderful painting that she has been trying to sell for the past 3 months, with no luck. The painting is about 11 September 2001. This day is very important to the Americans, more so than it is for other countries. After the research, she decides to get a nice expensive frame for the painting to give it more value, class and dignity and then sends it to a gallery in America for exhibit. She had figured out that it would be easier to sell the artwork in America, as the majority of people living there would be able to relate to the painting. This lady empowered herself and enhanced her art knowledge, by doing this research. By doing so, she invested in herself.

We as people are like seeds, seeds don't grow to produce good fruit if they are not nurtured. Money is also like a seed, it doesn't grow if it's not invested. Nothing grows to be rewarding if no value is added to it. I will share with you the things that are imperative for the growth of a successful entrepreneur. Things in which you need to personally invest, in order to be an extraordinary entrepreneur.

(a). **Invest in Knowledge:** There are certain facts that you should know about knowledge.
- By gaining more knowledge, you have the advantage of knowing more about business.
- You increase your understanding of situations, such as the economic climate.

Learn about marketing; learn what other people in business are doing. Also, learn about the mistakes other entrepreneurs make. My mathematics teacher once told me that a wise man learns from his mistakes, but a wiser man learns from other people's mistakes.

Out of all the things that I discuss here, I think the most important thing is increasing your knowledge and I would like to encourage you to invest more in cultivating your brain, through knowledge. The brain is a very powerful organ. In this book (in the chapter: Balancing Emotions, Stereotypes and reality) we spoke about the rational ruler. The rational ruler is the part of the brain that helps and guides us to reality, and helps us to make decisions that are not twisted. Knowledge is very important to enable us to make reasonable decisions.

(b). **Invest in a clean credit record:** A clean credit record is essential. You never know when you will need that credit. But also note that the credit that you make use of should be justified. Too much money going towards paying interest on unnecessary debts is a waste. You will never build your empire while wasting the little you have on interest, you need to ensure that any debt you have is necessary to grow your income and increase your net worth. Avoid debts that don't pay you back!

(c). **Invest in time management:** Stay organized. Many people lose deals because of procrastination and time wastage. There is no time like the present. If you have to pack a lunchbox for tomorrow at 9pm and you promise yourself that you will pack it tomorrow at 6am, you are giving yourself an excuse not to do it and you are lying to yourself. Such small things can make a difference to your life.

(d). **Invest in the art of negotiation:** Negotiation is the art of convincing another party to compromise, in order to reach a point beneficial to both parties. At some point, you might both end up having to compromise. It's a very handy skill and it works in all areas of your business. You need it for your suppliers, customers, employees and even willing investors.

- Suppliers may give discounts if you negotiate effectively.
- Customers may buy more. Also, customers who are struggling to pay you, are generally able to find a point of agreement when you negotiate with them. In the end, you at least get something back.
- Employees compromise and reach a point of agreement.
- Investors also find a mutual agreement and realise the benefits of investing, if the deal is negotiated properly.

(e). Invest in Innovations: This comes back to evolution, as mentioned in the previous chapter (your wealth is on customer retention). Teach yourself and your staff to come up with new ways to provide a service that is lucrative for both you and your customers.

(f). Invest in values: Every business needs to have values. Values such as integrity; treating your customers and staff fairly and being honest in all your business dealings.

You need to set values for your business and filter them to your staff. And most importantly, your values need to support your vision. They need to be a means to get to your company's vision.

CONCLUSION

Money is not everything; it is hard to obtain it and to grow it, without considering which other things you should invest in.

"If we start by growing ourselves as entrepreneurs, we get the

opportunity to embrace more responsibilities"   -- Siboniso Thwala

CHECKLIST

i.	Embracing Responsibility	✔
ii.	Playing a role	✔
iii.	Managing your brain	✔
iv.	Building and looking after strategies	✔
v.	Understanding the secrets of wealth	✔
vi.	Understanding simple investments	✔
vii.	Looking forward to the future	

More changes are coming.

I guarantee you that your bright future can be secured only if you are not bound by physical materials

7.MOBILITY IS POSSIBLY THE FUTURE OF BUSINESS

THE PHYSICAL MOBILITY OF BUSINESS

Besides my passion for writing and being an analyst, I also run a mobile catering business. I run this business using equipment which is suitable enough to enable me to move around offering my services. By catering I don't mean that I'm limited to cooking only, I also hire out, build and sell mobile kitchens on orders from people who are in the food business. I realised the future of mobility and took action, and I must say it's a lucrative business. Not only is it lucrative to me, but also to the person hiring, or buying, the mobile kitchen. Let us look at the advantages that motivate me to encourage mobility for your business.

Advantages of mobility

(a).   No expensive rentals or mortgage loans

When conducting a business in a building you are faced with many expenses, such as the monthly rental or bond repayments of the building. Such costs tend to compel businesses to overcharge for services and products. Maybe you have noticed that a sandwich bought from the more affluent side of town, is more expensive than a sandwich bought from the less affluent side of town. This is because the business owner has to factor his rental expenses into the price of his products. The products thus become more expensive to the customer. Ownership of a building comes with even more expenses,

83

such as municipal levies. Levies vary per area; again, the more classy the area, the more expensive the levy becomes.

(b).   The ability to migrate easily to greener pastures and keep up with change

When change happens in an environment, some animals are forced to migrate to find food and more favourable living and breeding conditions. In business, when change happens, entrepreneurs are sometimes forced to cut their costs and increase their prices, or even close their businesses. If mobility makes it possible for animals to survive, and achieve their needs and desires, why can't we learn to do that?

Only change is guaranteed in life and life is the driving essence to any form of business. This simply means that businesses are forced to shape up and fit into the changes and challenges that life presents. Even if your business is office based, mobility is the next step forward that you should introduce to your customers.

Imagine a situation where you own a shop next to a soccer stadium. You get support and make a good turn over, when there are big soccer matches at the stadium, because everyone knows you very well and they enjoy your food. Every month-end Saturday there are two soccer matches scheduled, one at midday, at the stadium close to your shop and another in the evening, at the stadium which is 15km away from your business. Well, chances are that you won't make money on the evening match. The reason is that no-one is prepared to travel back and forth to buy your food, when they have the alternative to buy from the shop near the other stadium. Yes, they might prefer your food, but it is inconvenient for them to travel so far. Your customers will thus be forced to buy from your competitor.

This shows that, although you might have a profitable shop run from a building, you might need to consider spicing up your business, by adding some mobility. Perhaps you should consider investing in a food trailer, or a mobile kitchen, to better serve the needs of your customers.

(c).   *Mobility offers you the chance to be known everywhere*

Apart from the opportunity to reduce your costs, mobility also offers a chance for your businesses to be known over a larger area, possibly even all over the world. Being known in many places, by many people, allows you to take advantage of more of the opportunities offered in your industry. This also creates more opportunities for customers to choose you, over other businesses which may not offer them the same standard of service, or product.

More marketing

Mobility has the advantage in that it is a fairly cost effective marketing tool. Your food trucks, mobile kitchens, wheel alignment trucks etc, offer more exposure for your business as they travel to and from assignments.

THE CAR WHEEL ALIGNMENT BUSINESS THAT STOLE MY HEART

I met a guy from Pakistan, who runs a wheel alignment business in the Johannesburg CBD. He started his business there, because he recognised that the people, who reside in the flats in the area, needed a wheel alignment service close by. After some time, once his business was established, he decided to expand the business by offering a mobile wheel alignment service.

All the material and equipment he requires to operate his mobile business is kept in a truck, which allows him to move whenever, and wherever, he is needed for the service. After deciding to go mobile in addition to operating from a building, his profits tripled, merely because going mobile offered him the chance to expose his wonderful service to the city. Some of his clients, who live further away, even choose to go to his building for the service if his truck is fully booked for the day. Do you think that many people, who have to travel out of their area, would have chosen to use his business if they only knew him through adverts, or even heard of him by word-of-mouth?

How did he triple his profits? After rendering outstanding service to his clients with his mobile truck, the clients decide to continue supporting his business.

This works very well for him and for the client, considering that time is always an important factor for people in their busy lives. With his mobile business, he is able to meet a client at work. This is offers convenience to a client who may be unable to leave his work premises due to work pressure, or being unable to get a leave of absence from his employer. The client also appreciates the time he saves by escaping the long hours waiting in queues.

COMMON CHALLENGES FOR MOBILE BUSINESSES

Running a mobile business may have some challenges, such as the travelling expenses which can be very high, if they are not planned for properly. For example, committing to conducting business in a remote area, without a secured payment, can be very costly. There are also several other challenges of which you need to be aware.

THE LAW

After spending a year and some months on my catering equipment business, I took the time to investigate some of the common challenges which are faced by the people to whom I have rented, or sold, catering equipment.

I dedicate this section to them and would like to thank them all for giving me the wisdom, knowledge and courage to help others. Once again, thank you all. Others will succeed tomorrow because of you!

The law is the most common challenge which causes people to give up on mobility, especially the mobile businesses that trade as street vendors. Besides meeting clients at their premises to conduct and conclude business, you might want to further offer your services as a street vendor. Therefore, in order to more fully equip you in the mobile trading business, I would like to take this opportunity to enlighten you on the laws of street vending. Mobile trading may require you to conduct your business on the street; therefore it is imperative for you to have some background on the requirements for street trading.

Street trading is governed by bylaws and each city has its own bylaws, depending on where you want to conduct your business. I've investigated the bylaws in South Africa and I have to tell you that every province and region has its own. I have therefore chosen to focus on the ones which are most common to all the provinces. In addition to this, I would encourage you to request that your provincial municipality provides you with any additional information on these bylaws, before you begin trading as a mobile trader and especially as a street vendor. If you live and work outside of South Africa, please note that the laws stipulated below may not be relevant to you, so you also, will need to contact your provincial legislature for the bylaws applicable to you. Some provinces and regions with additional public areas, such as beaches, will have additional bylaws for such areas.

Fortunately, for some cities and provinces, the bylaws are available on the internet and you can use the Google search engine to obtain them.

The laws of informal street vending

The most important prevention, against failure in business, is to know your rights and be aware of any actions that might lead you to the wrong side of the law and thus jeopardise your venture. Yes, basically the does and don'ts. The informal trading bylaws have been agreed on and written to regulate informal trading within the jurisdictional area of the city, in a manner that recognises and enhances the city's constitutional and other statutory obligations. These laws relate to all forms of informal trading;

Forms of informal trading

- Street trading, which comprises the selling of goods, or supplying of services for reward, in a public road;
- Selling of goods in a Linear Market;
- Sale of goods or services in a public place;
- Mobile trading from caravans and light motor vehicles;

- Selling of goods in stalls or kiosks;
- Selling of goods at special events.

Anyone, who is a member of the community, may enter into informal trading, as stipulated by our law, subject to compliance with the provision of the Bylaw, the Act and any other applicable law.

What are bylaws?

They are rules and regulations written to govern an organisation. Commonly, they may specify the qualifications, rights, duties and liabilities of an organisation. Every region in South Africa has bylaws which are applicable to it.

The following are the most common bylaws taken from the Provincial Gazette.

These bylaws prohibit an informal trader from:-

- Trading in a garden to which the public has right of access;
- Trading directly alongside the following;
- A building belonging to the SA police or a police station;
- A church, mosque, synagogue or any other place of worship;
- A building declared to be a public monument;
- A bank automated teller machine (ATM)
- Informal trading may not occur in a place where it causes an obstruction in respect of a fire hydrant, or any entrance or exit from a building, or where it is likely to obstruct traffic;
- Trading on the half of a road adjacent to a building used for residential property; if the owner or occupier of the building objects and if that objection is raised to the informal trader by an authorised official (being the official of the council, traffic officer, member of police service or peace officer);

- Trading within 5 meters of any intersection;
- On a sidewalk attached to the building of any person who sells similar goods to that being sold on the sidewalk by the informal trader, if the trader is selling the goods without the prior consent of the person selling similar goods in the building and if the authorised official raises the fact that consent from the person selling similar goods does not exist.

These bylaws restrict an informal trader from:-

- Sleeping overnight at the place where he/she conducts informal trading;
- Erecting any structure for the purpose of providing a shelter, unless approved by the council;
- Placing a property in a public place. The motor vehicle or trailer which is used for his / her informal trading is the exception, provided that it doesn't hinder the movement of pedestrians or vehicles. Also it must comply with the provisions of the traffic act;
- Selling or promotion of alcoholic products, if permitted to trade on the beach;
- Use of bells, hooters, amplified equipment or similar devices which emit sounds, in order to attract customers, while trading on the beach;
- You are prohibited from using any form of electrical supply, or power generator, unless expressly approved and provided for in the relevant permit.

Further to this information; The provincial gazette promotes hygiene, in and around the area where the informal trader is conducting business. It stipulates that the informal trader must collect all refuse; scrap or waste material produced while trading and deposit it into a suitable refuse repository. Such must be done on a daily basis at the end of trading.

THE MOBILITY OF MONEY

Technology is shrinking the use of physical cash

When we were growing up, we heard stories of people collecting pay cheques in envelopes, senior citizens collecting pensions from cashiers at government offices and businesses collecting debts by going door-to-door. Now things have changed; people get paid via bank transfers, payment of debt gets facilitated by debit orders, stop orders, EFT payments, and so on.

What is the future of money?

Can you see that people are trying to cut down on reckless spending?

Can you see the link between people's desire to spend wisely and the support from technology?

Yeah, technology is strongly facilitating the mobility of money.

The motive behind technology support

Globally, people have gotten wise, and so they want to track how much of their money is going where. Plastic money, in form of bank cards, has made it easier for people to accurately watch their spending habits. This helps them to;

- Eliminate the surprises on their budget variances,

- Keep them in line with their credit spending and affordability.

Plastic money, linked to a banking account, makes possible purchases, and payments for goods and services, by debit or credit card. Banking technology, in the form of account spending records, or statements, allows clients to track all payments made into and out of their accounts, when using either these cards, or doing transfers via internet banking. The Banks encourage people to use these facilities as it is a win-win situation for all concerned.

Banks also encourage this technology because it aids in cutting costs in many areas, such as;

- Eliminating accounting errors made by employees and the cost thereof,
- Salaries of people processing and approving transactions,
- Rental and building maintenance costs. Electronic banking reduces the need for branches where rent, maintenance costs and salaries have to be paid. This translates into a saving for the customer through a reduction in banking charges.

More win for the client because of;

- The bank saves money and the client saves on charges; the banks give discounts on charges to clients for utilising technology instead of doing physical banking.
- The client has access to a permanent electronic record of all transactions on his account.
- Clients are more empowered to save money by keeping track of their spending to ensure that they operate within their budgets.

This only teaches us

- As entrepreneurs we also need to assist our clients to save on expenses. For example, perhaps what you save in banking charges can be given back to your customers in discounts.
- Realise that if you don't do this, someone else will and they will cash in on it.
- It shows us that, as business people, we need to be sensitive to the pockets of our clients. We can also benefit from assisting our clients to save money.
- The more we offer clients options to spend less, the more we will benefit from them.

Mobile Money benefits for your business

(a). Cutting long queues

Your clients have a lot taking up their time these days, things such as watching favourite TV programs, assisting kids with their homework, taking work home, fulfilling their career dreams by studying after work and so on. You can't expect them to waste their precious time by having to queue at an ATM to get cash, in order to buy from you, then after that still queue to buy your services and products. Why should it be a hustle to support you? Many businesses lose money for this reason. Do you know that it costs a client more money to withdraw from a credit card than to buy directly with it? This could perhaps be the reason why your most loyal customer didn't buy from you today!

(b). No necessity to keep cash for change

As clients buy from you, from time to time a transaction will require change. Trust me; you don't want to cancel a transaction because you don't have change. You don't want to turn away a client because you don't have change.

(c). More effective bookkeeping

It's easier to measure cash flow when your receipts and expenses reflect on your bank statements. Another benefit of this is that it is also easier for creditors to measure your cash flow, should you ever require credit.

(d). Theft prevention

Physical cash is a bigger risk for theft. You don't want your employees, or any criminals out there, to be tempted to steal your hard earned cash. If you have to have a cash trade, in addition to an electronic one, it's safer to have a smaller portion of it physically available and the rest of it in a bank account.

What you need to do

Speak to your bank of choice and find out more. You can hire speed points for swiping, or have them added as part of your account package. You can also apply for the facility to allow clients to transfer money from their cell phones.

There are many methods of making and receiving payments, don't chase the paper, chase the value! Money is getting more mobile and from what I can tell, sometime in the future, even if it's in a hundred years or more when I am longer around, there will be no further need for printing money because it's only the value that counts, not the paper!

CONCLUSION

In spite of all these challenges, I still see a future for mobility. I believe that there are many more improvements that can be made, to the mobile market, in terms of the mobile services offered. There are plenty of businesses that can easily fit into the mobile market; it doesn't have to be limited to the examples I used.

MY PROPHECY

Clients will slowly move away from physical money and chase after service. Money will become even more mobile and no-one will need to travel anywhere to buy goods and services; instead, the goods and services will need to travel to them. In the future, there will be no need for cash as all businesses will use mobile electronic facilities. Clients will be able to sit at home, as businesses become more and more mobile in their service delivery, and so enjoy a comfortable life being served as kings and queens.

CHECKLIST

i.	**Embracing Responsibility**	✔	
ii.	**Playing a role**	✔	
iii.	**Managing your brain**	✔	
iv.	**Building and looking after strategies**	✔	
v.	**Understanding the secrets of wealth**		✔
vi.	**Understanding simple investments**	✔	
vii.	**Looking forward to the future**		✔

EPILOGUE

WE ARE INDEBTED TO THE RESPONSIBILITY WHICH WE EMBRACE

For clients to remain loyal to us as entrepreneurs, we need to be aware of the fact that we have a great responsibility towards enabling them to live the life that they want to live.

To trigger that responsibility, please always remember the following:

- There is a symbiotic relationship between the ones who can and the disabled. The ones, who are able to do something, will benefit from the deed just as much as the ones who are disabled.
- Once that responsibility is embraced, the entrepreneur needs to be aware of the life time responsibility. A role of the entrepreneur is a lifetime responsibility, once embraced it's not easy to escape. It's like giving birth to a baby and vouching to live up to the expectations thereafter!
- An entrepreneur needs to relate business scenarios to simple daily life situations in order to find beneficial solutions.
- Value your strategy as an asset. There is no need to be frustrated by scarcity and lack of resources; even when you can only crawl, you can still get from point A to point B.
- Managing and understanding the power of emotion is an important tool in striving toward success.

97

- Becoming successful can be easy if you commit to the trust equation and understanding the principles of wealth.
- It is essential to take the time to invest in growing yourself and your employees rather than only focusing on the money. Money follows after. If we grow ourselves, we also have an opportunity to grow our customers.
- Entrepreneurs need to embrace change, because change is inevitable and resisting it is just going to sink your business.
- Value the time of your customers. Everyone wants to save time and money so it is a good idea to keep in mind that time costs money.
- People are feeling more important these days, so treat them like kings and queens and you will be well on your way to becoming legendary.

I wish you all the best in your endeavours toward success!

Please get in touch with Siboniso should you have any comments: info@sibonisothwala.com.

8. LIST OF REFERENCES

1. https://www.insighthealthcare.org/our-services/talking-therapies/nottingham/types-of-difficulties/low-self-esteem/
2. http://www.suzeorman.com/files/2914/1562/6541/SuzesStory2014.pdf
3. http://mute-net.sourceforge.net/howAnts.shtml
4. http://www.joburg.org.za/images/stories/2012/Sept/local_government_-_municipal_systems_act_32-2000_-_city_of_johannesburg_-_informal_trading_by-laws_final%20%20by%20laws%203.pdf
5. http://www.capetown.gov.za/en/ByLaws/Draft%20bylaws/Draft%20bylaw%20informal%20trading.pdf
6. https://www.quora.com/How-do-ants-sense-food
7. https://en.wikipedia.org/wiki/Ant